To my heartbeats Shelomi and Ishuah,
my niecege & nephages
&
all Giddy readers everywhere

Did you know Hippos can open their mouths to 150 degrees or 4 feet wide?

First published in Great Britain in 2019 by Giddy Moose. Leg8cy House, 17 Featherbank Mount, LS18 4QL. Text and Illustrations © J c Love & Giddy Moose 2013. Illustrator: Stefan Filotti. The rights of Giddy Moose, Jc Love, to be identified as the author and owner of this work has been asserted by them in accordance with the copyright, Designs and Patent Act, 1988. All rights reserved. Printed in the UK

A cip catalogue record for this book is available from the British Library.

ISBN 978-1-909944-00-8
www.Giddymoose.com

The Longest Yawn

A *tremendously tantalising tongue twisting tale*

Note for readers:
The Giddymoose comma fatigue panel has authorised the removal of many commas due to be present in this book. Please be aware, all commas in question have now secured suitable Giddy accomodation elsewhere..

One way to read this book:
Read each page aloud as quickly and correctly as you can. Can you read the whole book without having to start a sentence again?

Practice makes perfect!

Giddymoose & Stefan Filotti

Hippo's water pool rippled fiercely with shimmering, toxic bubbles of mud. A disgusting scent filled the air and Hippo sat up straight and grunted loudly.

At times, Hippo could be very ill-tempered and cantankerous. He detested anyone visiting his muddy water pool without an invitation.

He loudly belched and broke wind without saying "pardon" or "excuse me". He purposely picked his nostrils if anyone spoke to him, and often chased visitors away.

After a while, visitors learned to stay away from Hippo's territory. His days became quiet and tranquil, but Hippo was utterly bored. Every morning he followed his usual humdrum routine.

He sprawled lazily in his mudpool, closed his eyes and opened his mouth as wide as he could YAWN.

First, Hippo's yawn stretched wide enough to swallow a leprechaun.

Then, wide enough to swallow a sea monster.

Soon, it was wide enough to swallow a basketball-playing dragon.

Immediately, as Hippo began to yawn,

Three truly tireless turtles tripped the selfish shellfish with three twisted thick tightly twined twigs twittering, "He threw three free throws, he threw three free throws!"

Shortly afterwards,

four frantically fearful frogs fled from five fierce furry fruit flies, as five fresh fish furiously floundered flipping their fins, faking flying fishes.

a prancing pleasant plucky pheasant passionately parading, who paused patiently preening his perfectly positioned plumage, profusely persuading "please pay promptly! please pay promptly!"

Immediately after the pheasant won the dance battle,

many massive muscular moodily-moving muddy maggots meekly munched mouldy mashed moist mixed mushrooms.

And...

A crammed crate of clattering clean clams confronted by a cunning camel keenly chewing a creamy caramel candy-cane continually cautioned,

"any noise annoys an oyster, but a noisy noise annoys an oyster more!"

But, Hippo couldn't hear the commotion because his ears were muffled while he yawned.

By the afternoon, Hippo's mouth had stretched to an angle of nearly one hundred and fifty degrees.
His large curved canines were on full display as he yawned to the sky - utterly bored.

Meanwhile, a wide weathered wise wriggling whale watching and waiting by the water wittily wrote, 'many an anemone sees an enemy anemone,'

In a tree nearby, a lonely large lightly laughing leopard leaning lopsidedly, literally longing for a lemon and lime lolly listlessly lisped,

"Red lorry, yellow lorry, red lorry, yellow lorry
Red lorry, yellow lorry, red lorry, yellow lorry!"

Later, just before darkness fell across the water pool and Hippo finally finished yawning...

Sitting up in his pool, Hippo sighed deeply, jiggled his jaw and smacked his lips together as his stomach rumbled. It was time to eat.

Hippo grazed hungrily. It had been another dull and boring day. Tomorrow he hoped, would be better.

After a last rapidly released rancid and unrefined wind, Hippo admired the toxic mud bubbles before falling fast asleep.

See our Giddymoose books

Anansi and the Moruga Scorpions

The Rotten tooth fairy

Binky The Angel Orb and the Morg

Time for Bed

Squeebit

Harry won't listen

Giddymoose.com

Twitter@TheGiddymoose

Instagram@TheGiddymoose

Z